What's your type?

I bet it's the Cooper Black!
with its Rounded Serifs
and Long Ascenders

It Seduces
It's Hot, it's Sexy
It's Big, Black and Beautiful

from Sheer Ugliness

BIG
Black
&
Beautiful

Cooper Black book

Executive Editor
Art Director
Ward Nicolaas
www.cafe-open.com

Editors
Graphic Design
Karin ter Laak
Charlotte Aal

Copy
Ellen Ter Beek

Proofreader
Joy Maul-Phillips

Publisher
BIS Publishers
Building Het Sieraad
Postjesweg 1
1057 DT Amsterdam
The Netherlands

T (31) 020 515 02 30
F (31) 020 515 02 39

bis@bispublishers.nl
www.bispublishers.nl

BIG Black & Beautiful

Cooper Black book

Ward Nicolaas

BIS

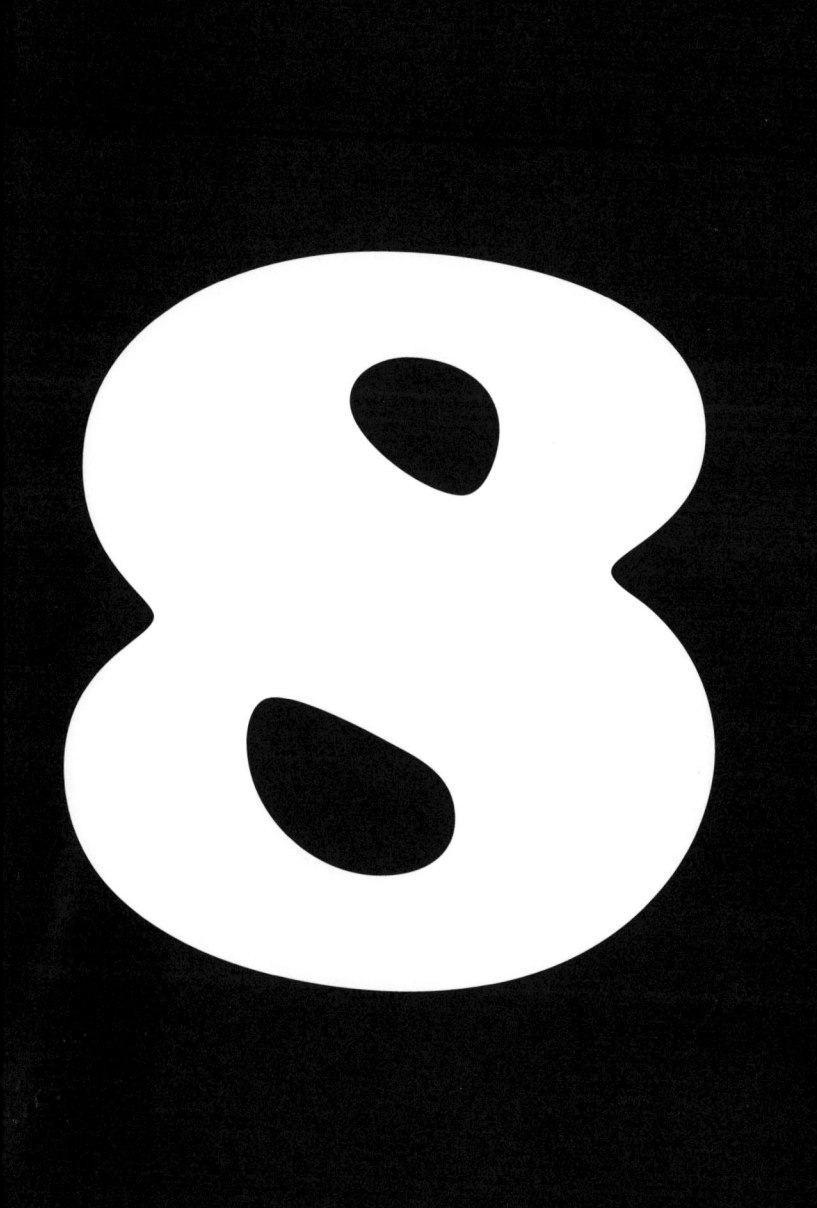

Pref

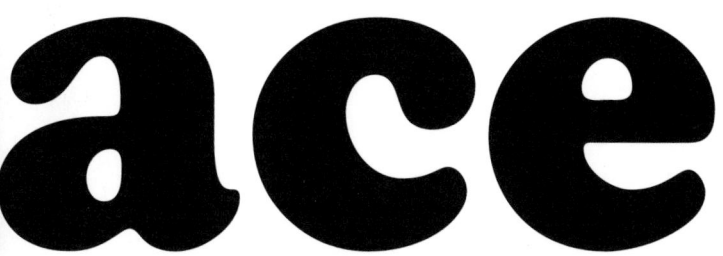

Admiring Cooper Black is like being the most popular kid in school and falling in love with the ugliest person in the class. Sharing this secret, telling people — your friends — about it is hard, and must be done gradually, little by little, until you are comfortable enough to be seen in public together - holding hands, laughing, kissing, using Cooper Black.

At the beginning there will be guilt and shame. Some mockery is to be expected, but the rewards will be many and the pleasures enormous. The first step in fully understanding Cooper Black is to accept the fact that it is ugly: sexy ugly. There is no reason to feel attracted to it at first glance. The proportions are bizarre, the serifs are some crossbreed of whale and polar bear, its weight is too heavy at minimum and the 'o' is tilted beyond belief.

How then, can a typeface with so much against it be so popular? So coveted and desired? That's easy to answer. Cooper Black has personality, charisma, love. It's jovial, good-natured, approachable. It is surprising, turning up in the strangest places: dentists' offices, laundromats, restaurants, markets, gift shops. Everywhere. Everyday. In our lives. It's Cooper Black.

by Armin Vit
UnderConsideration
<u>www.underconsideration.com</u>

19

22

A ti

ne...

wh
you co
a man

en
ld call
man...

wh
the pape
served at t
and
only bit i

en
was still
e doorstep
logs
urglars...

wi
wearing a
could make
without
in your

en
sturdy hat
you survive
a penny
pocket.

That year...

Cooper Black
entered the
world stage and
turned a word into
a gesture just by its
looks; *the* undeniable
pokerface of all
typefaces.

Photogr

Oswald Cooper

△ source **The Book of Oz Cooper An Appreciation of Oswald Bruce Cooper** edited by **Raymond DaBoll** publisher **Society of Typographic Arts, Chicago, 1949** picture by **Justin Craigen**

Dear Oz,

THA
YO

ANK
OU!

AMPERSANDS

&	&	&	&	&
&	&	&	&	&
&	&	&	&	&
&	&	&	&	
&	Like many typographic designers, Cooper loved to play with the flexible ampersand. Most of these are reproduced directly from Cooper copy but it was found necessary to redraw several from tracings.		&	

Oswald Cooper

1879–1940

The passing of Oswald Cooper leaves for many of us an unfillable void. Where can we turn in these days to find another truly great man so utterly unimpressed by his own importance?

The story of Cooper has a definite homespun quality. It is no mere coincidence that various people in speaking or writing of Cooper have mentioned his likeness to Lincoln, for there was much about him that was reminiscent of 'the Great Emancipator' — not only his long, lanky figure and homely, lovable face, but his kindly nature, his dislike of ostentation, and his quaint, dry humor.

He was born on April 13, 1879, in Mount Gilead, Ohio; later the family moved to Coffeyville, Kansas, where he attended grammar and high school. At the age of 16 he forsook high school to become a printer's devil in a local newspaper and job printing shop. Five years later he came to Chicago and entered the Frank Holme Art School. Here one of his fellow students was a young chap named W.A. Dwiggins, their teacher was Frederic W. Goudy — three names destined to be 'tops' in their field.

In this same school Cooper first met Fred Bertsch and upon leaving school these two formed a partnership, their intention being to open a type shop and set type as it should be set. But finding that type cost money, a commodity on which they happened to be short, they were forced to turn out complete advertisements in hand-lettering and hand-drawn borders with Cooper doing the lettering and Bertsch the borders. As they began to gain recognition more important things came their way they did entire campaigns for the Packard Motor Car Company, for Atkinson, Mentzer & Company (school books), and for Anheuser-Busch.

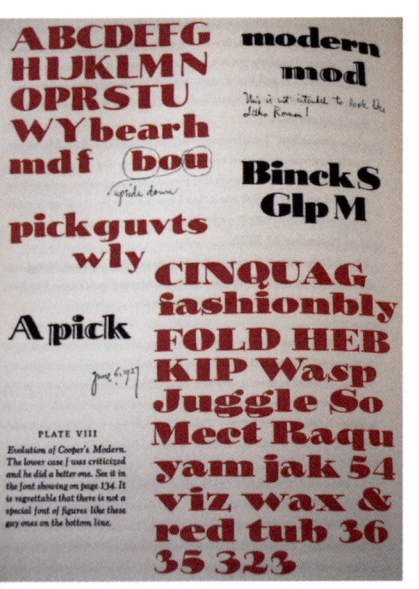

PLATE VIII
Evolution of Cooper's Modern. The lower case I was criticized and he did a better one. See it in the font showing on page 134. It is regrettable that there is not a special font of figures like these gay ones on the bottom line.

The vigorous character of Cooper's drawn letters, and the freshness and strength of his arrangements, soon set his work apart as truly distinguished advertising. The Cooper style became the star to which young lettering men tried to hitch their wagons. His influence in the graphic arts field was far greater than that of many better known artists. Entirely unself-seeking, he preferred a sort of cloistered life and his prominence was gained chiefly by the 'better mouse trap' method. Back in the early days of Bertsch & Cooper, Fred Bertsch's dramatic selling of his idol, 'Ozzie', made many an advertising man conscious of the existence of this remarkable, but unseen personality. Even without publicity his influence

would have been felt, for the lettering men and designers were acutely conscious of 'Ozzie.' His mastery of design in layout made his work the envy and despair of these hard working craftsmen and set standards difficult to attain. Probably no present-day lettering man has been more imitated, with the possible exception of Dwiggins. Even the type founders copied Cooper letter forms. (The Packard face was based on his style as developed in Packard ads.)

Fred S. Bertsch
& Oswald Cooper
ten years at Room 718
Athenaeum Building
59 E. Van Buren Street
have moved across
the hall to Room 703
and they have a new
telephone number
Harrison 5889

May
1914

Harrison
7771

Bertsch & Cooper
have a new telephone
number. Or you can
call Harrison 7772—
for they now have
two (2) lines (Mercy!)
and a switchboard
(Imagine!)—a regula
"private exchange
all departments.
(Well, forevermore!

15th Year
at 59 E. Van Buren St.
(How time flies!)

Bertsch & Cooper
Designers · Typographers
59 E. Van Buren St. Chicago

For

f 63

38

As Cooper's reputation grew the partnership prospered, and at last the long dreamed of type shop became a reality. A short time later that meticulous and indefatigable typographer, Edwin B. Gillespie, became a partner and was placed in charge of the shop. Then, being able to handle a greater volume of work, it gradually became necessary to build up their design department. The favored few who thus had the privilege of intimate contact with Cooper were fortunate indeed — these men: Kleboe, Riley, Plate, Drewry, Player, Parley, Lerner, Edgar Miller, Ressinger, DaBoll, McCray, Vlasaty and others not only gained in ability under the Cooper tutelage, but also had that rarer experience of working with a great master whose most outstanding characteristic was his complete humility.

Later came the heyday in advertising. Illustrators were added to the staff. First Joe Chenoweth — Myron Perley became a partner for a time — then Millhauser, Mayo Bunker, Jeff Grant and Frank Raymond. It was in the midst of these strenuous times that the capable young Suzanne Hotze suddenly discovered herself no longer the mere office girl she had been hired to be, but actually the business manager of a fast-moving enterprise. Then Charles Everett Johnson became a partner and brought into the fold almost all the top ranking artists in the Middle West. Under one roof was such a galaxy of stars as Andy Loomis, Harry Timmins, Phil Lyford, Roy Spreter, Frank Mayfield, Carl Neher, Haddon Sundblom, and others.

Cooper's whimsical humor probably did more to endear him to us than any other trait. His Christmas cards, drawn as only Cooper could draw them, are collectors' items.

Each a gem of masterful whimsy, they are perhaps even more treasured for his writing than for the beautiful free rendering. His ability as a writer again is evidenced in the advertising pieces produced on rare occasions for his firm, and in the introductory notes and specimen sheets for the various typefaces he designed. Contrasting in pleasant relief against that sea of braggadocio: the usual vain-glorious advertising, these announcements shone out by their disarming frankness, their restraint and understatement, with always a final quirk of sparkling humor. Advertising agencies bid for his services as a copy writer — from one, at least, he had a standing offer — but to all of this he turned a deaf ear.

ABCDEFGHIJKL
NOPQRSTUVWXYZ&
abcdefghijklmnopq
rstuvwxyz
1234567890$
• · — . , ' : ; ! ? [ ]

...e early 19th century an English ty...
...der, Robert Thorne, cut a number ...
...vy black roman and italic faces whi...
... a considerable vogue in his day. Son...
...hese early 19th century types ha...
... revived and contemporary varieti...
...eavy black faces have been designe...

Many of us treasure in our files little workaday notes in the handwriting of 'Oz'. Usually they had come attached to a sheaf of proofs in the midst of a hectic rush and like a fresh breeze brought us back to a moment of sanity by that quaint, whimsical touch. Now that he is gone we'll treasure these relics all the more. Having known and worked with one such rare personality, it is too much to expect that we could be so fortunate again.

There is no replacing Oswald Cooper.

Harry H.Farrell

This tribute to Oswald Cooper first appeared in
The Bulletin of the Chicago Guild of Freelance Artists.

All images are from **The Book of Oz Cooper An Appreciation of Oswald Bruce Cooper**
edited by **Raymond DaBoll** publisher **Society of Typographic Arts, Chicago, 1949**
pictures by **Justin Craigen**
This book, replete with human as well as technical interest, includes reminiscences and tributes
by Frederic W. Goudy, W.A. Dwiggins, Gustave Baumann, Paul Standard and R.N. McArthur.

Ah, Coo

"Ah, Cooper. Isn't it interesting how we selectively associate a font with positive or negative visual icons? In the 1980s, I thought of Cooper as a dated 1970s font associated with those custom fuzzy-lettered T-shirts which were far out of fashion. In the early 1990s it was the overused vinyl cut graphics font. Later, it was remembered fondly as the Beach Boys *Pet Sounds* font and those T-shirts were back in style. Are we fated to fall in and out of love with Cooper Black until the end of time?"

by Ray Larabie
Typodermic Fonts
www.typodermic.com

Wh
so Fr

at's

nny?

HOLT EUCH

der leckeren

RUCHT KUGELN

10
Euro
Cent

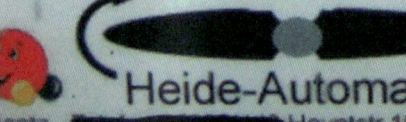

Heide-Automaten

Plantz · Telefon 05000 / 25 Hauptstr. 10 29392 Wesendorf

haltsstoffe: Zucker,GumBase,Glucosesirup,Aromastoffe,Farbstoffe
und Antioxodationsmittel E-3 auch für Diabetiker geeignet!

It's Hilarious

It's Harmless

It's Optimistic

It's Kiddish

It's Playful

It's a Happy Face

All Joy,
no Sorrow

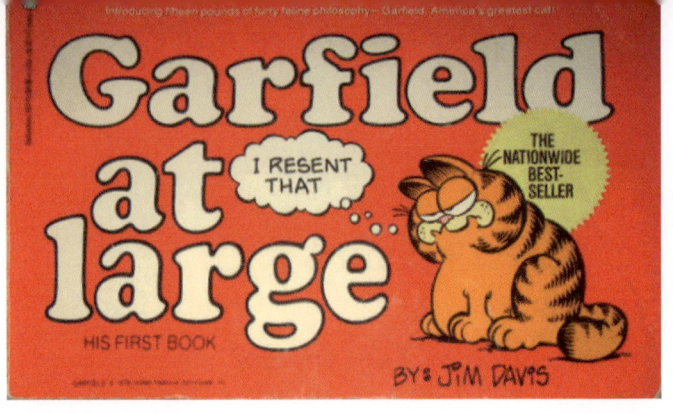

△ publisher **Ballantine Books**

▽ **Japan** picture by **Akira Yoshino**

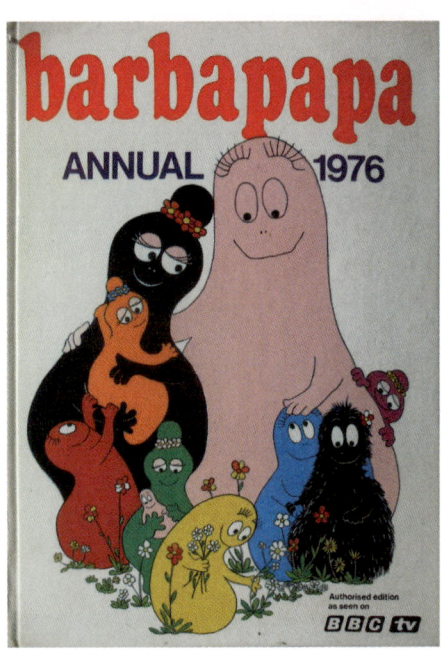

△ publisher **World Distributors LTD.**

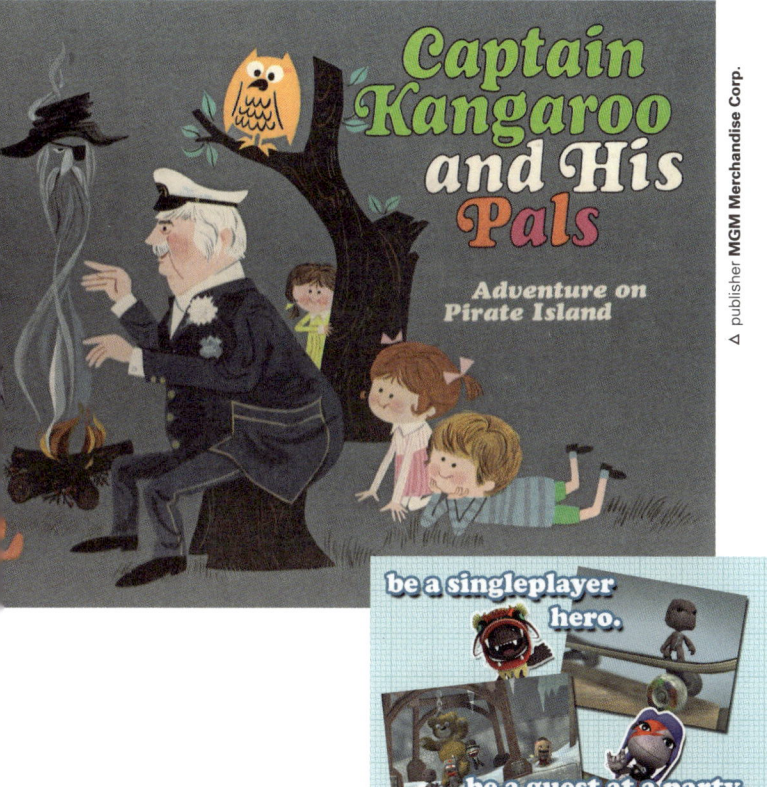

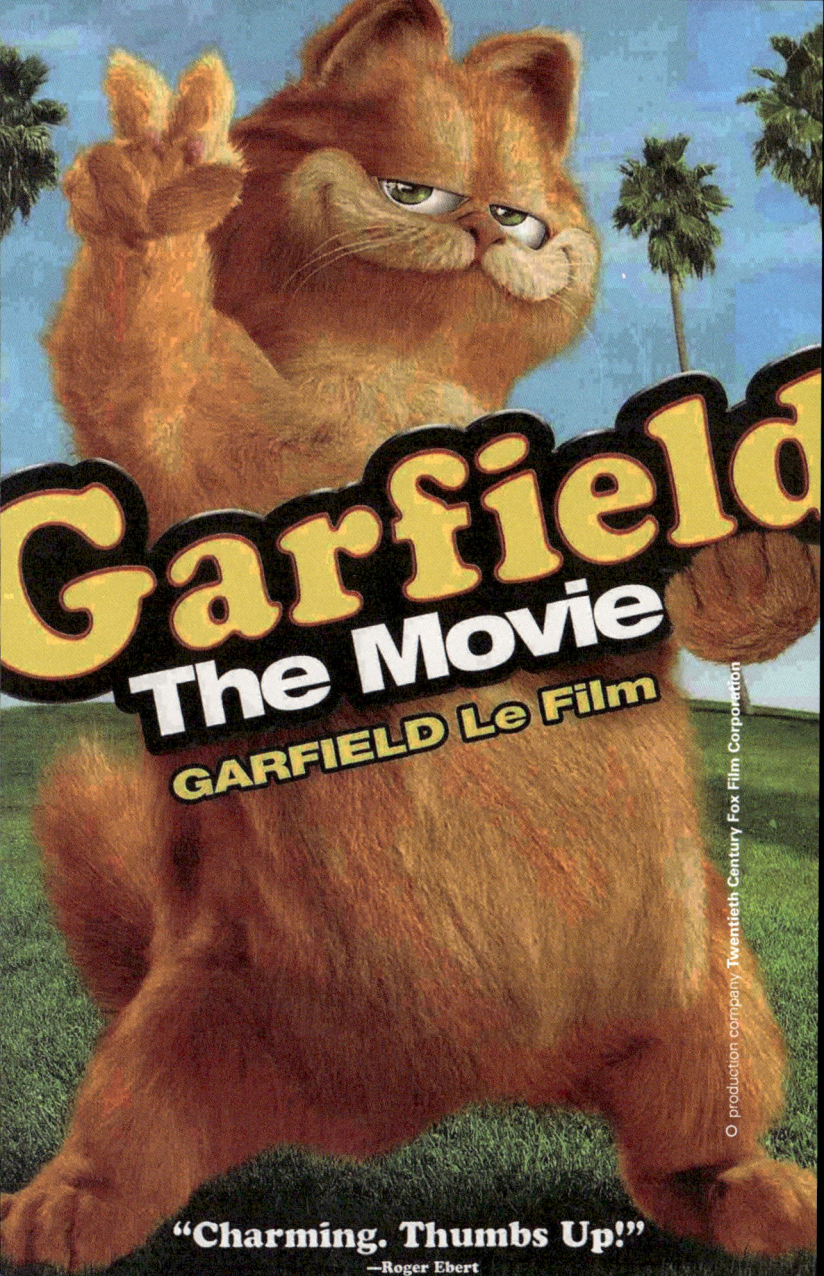

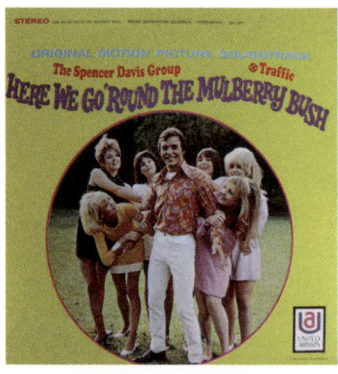

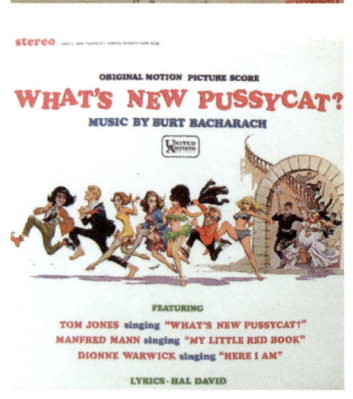

▽ The Netherlands picture by **Ward Nicolaas**

YOU C

SHAKING HANDS

KISSING

▽ source **Unknown**

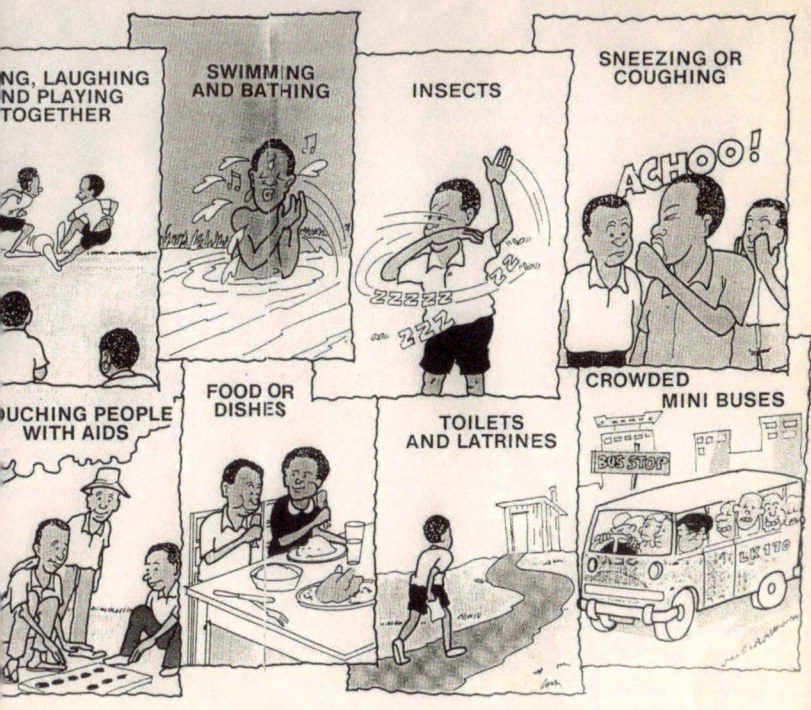

OUR H
PAT CO

ERO...
OPER

M*A*S*H

A JACK ROLLINS · CHARLES H. JOFFE Production

woody allen's
"bananas"

○ **Switzerland** picture by **Adam Tappman**

△ **United States** picture by **Adam Tappman**

▽ **Thailand** picture by **Ben Mitchell**

กลิ่นสตรอเบอร์รี่
โคลลอน
いちごコロン
บิสกิตโรล

Hello, Ceil
It's Me!!!
Betty Walker

PARAMOUNT PICTURES
presents

**Jack
Lemmon**
and
**Walter
Matthau**
are
**The
Odd
Couple**

...say
no
more.

Produced by HOWARD W. KOCH · Directed by GENE SAKS · Screenplay by NEIL SIMON Based on his play
Music NEAL HEFTI · A HOWARD W. KOCH Production · PANAVISION® TECHNICOLOR® A PARAMOUNT PICTURE

Wh
so S

at's
exy?

It's Voluptuous

It's Smooth

It's Fleshy

It's Soft

It's Black

It's in your Face

**All Meat,
no Bones**

Emmanuelle

X was never like this.

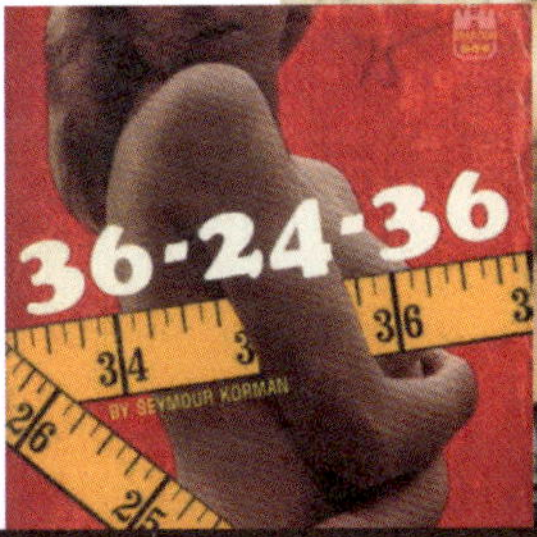

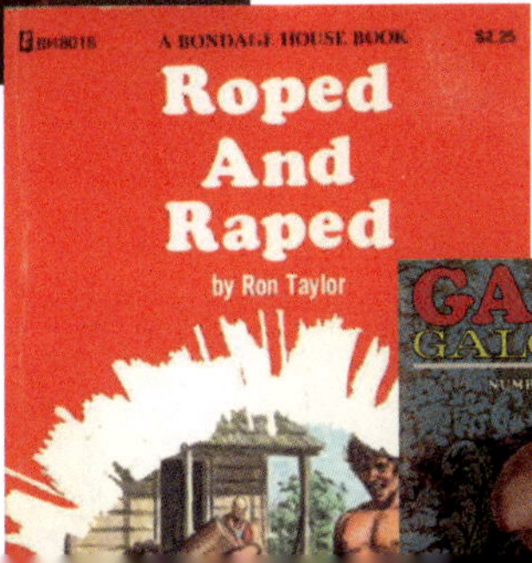

HOT PUSSIES AND

36-24-36

3|4   3|6   3

BY SEYMOUR KORMAN

ADULT WORLD
$5.00

COLD SPIKES
ANNUAL NO.

FROM ENGLAND!
HIGH HEEL SEX
PARADE WITH
PUSSIES GALORE

LIKE A MOTH TO A

All models

you

L.500

RIVIVONO LE
ORGIE ROMANE

AMORE
FRA DONNE

LA SFINGE
INNAMORATA

NOBILTA' VERSO
IL NUDO

DALLA RUSSIA
CON AMORE

SPED. IN ABB. POST. GR. III

BAC203 $3.95
Golden
Shower
Summer
by F. W. Lose

B RB8016   A BONDAGE HOUSE BOOK $2.35
Roped
And
Raped
by Ron Taylor

HE WORRIED ABOUT GLORIA'S MORALS.
IT NEVER OCCURRED TO HIM TO WORRY
ABOUT HIS OWN!

NEIGHBORLY
LOVER

BY
PETER
KANTO

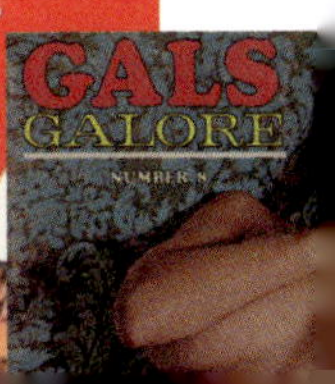

GALS
GALORE
NUMBER

△ **United States** picture by **John Hubbard**

△ **Japan** picture by **Adam Tappman**

SUBSCRIBE TO PLAYBOY NOW

Pay by check, postal draft, money order or currency of your country. Sorry —but no credit orders may be accepted.

Send your order to the address below most convenient to you:

PLAYBOY
c/o PLAYBOY Enterprises
3, Montpelier Square
London S.W. 7, England

PLAYBOY
232 E. Ohio St.
Chicago, Illinois 60611
U.S.A.

PLAYBOY's Special Foreign Rates

Europe	$12.60 or
British Isles	£4.10.0
Bel., Lux.	627 BFRS.
Denmark	87 DKR.
Finland	40.00 FMKS.
France	61.73 NF.
Greece	376 DR.
Ireland	90/-
Italy	7865 LIRE
Netherlands	45.47 FL.
Norway	90 NKR.
Portugal	360 ESC.
Spain	750 PTAS.
Sweden	64.74 SKR.
Switzerland	54.38 SFRS.
APO, FPO	$12.60

Other Countries	$15.60 or
Austria	400 SCH.
British Poss.	£5.10.0
Egypt	672 P.
French Poss.	76.43 NF.
Germany	65 DM.
Iraq	5.56 I.D.
Israel	46.57 I.L.
Japan	5581 YEN
Lebanon	48.75 L.L.
Saudi Arabia	69.96 RIALS
South Africa	11.43 RANDS
Turkey	140 T.L.
U.S., U.S. Poss., Canada & Pan-Am Union	$8

Printed in U.S.A.

subscribe to
PLAYBOY®
SPECIAL RATES FOR FOREIGN SUBSCRIBERS

one full year,
12
big issues

SAVE 20% OVER THE SINGLE-COPY PRICE

Please enter my subscription to PLAYBOY. I am enclosing check, postal draft, money order or currency in proper amount for my country as shown on reverse side of this card. *For example:* British Isles, £4.10.0; France, 61.73 NF.; Italy, 7865 Lire; Germany, 65 DM; Switzerland, 54.38 SFRS, etc.

FILL OUT AND MAIL THIS CARD   ☐ NEW OR   ☐ RENEWAL
to address on reverse side most convenient to you.

Your Name_____
                              (please print)

Address_____

City_____State or Province_____Country_____

Amount enclosed_____. (See over for correct amount required in funds of your country. All orders must be accompanied by full payment.)

☐ Check here if you would like information regarding Charter Key Privileges in the Playboy Club. First Club is scheduled to open in London soon.

B997

Muscle Up...

TO A HANDSOME BODY! START NOW WITH THESE

2 Free Muscle Building Gifts

MR. UNIVERSE IS A WEIDER PUPIL!

Dave Draper, a former fat boy, "Muscled-Up" with the Weider System—now is a star of movies, TV and is a "Mr. Universe" winner! WHY NOT YOU?

Gift 1

DIAL-A-BODY WHEEL—
One quick turn of this wheel shows you how to build Bigger Arms, Deeper Chest, Broader Shoulders. Makes Muscle Building more FUN!

ABSOLUTELY FREE!

ABSOLUTELY FREE!

Gift 2

HOW TO BUILD A STRONG MUSCULAR BODY!
Here the champs talk directly to you on how you, too can use their secrets to build yourself a strong muscular body. 32 pages crammed full of photos and muscle building tips!

ADD 3 INCHES TO YOUR ARMS 4 TO YOUR CHEST . . . IN 30 DAYS!
Secrets of the Champs Revealed!

This year alone, my Triple Progressive Muscle-Building System has developed winners of "Mr. America," "Mr. World," "Mr. Universe," "Mr. Europe," "Mr. Canada" and hundreds of other top "perfect man" titles . . . and I've been doing this year after year since 1936. That's a fact—I don't offer you lies, promises, isometric gadgets and useless exercisers but proven fitness and muscle-building techniques that have stood the test of time . . . and that have been successfully turning out champs for over 30 years. NOW!—I'm ready to **send you 2 FREE GIFTS** — to prove to you that in just 15-minutes-a-day you will be fit, get into athletic shape or build a powerful, champion-building body! In the privacy of your own home you can quickly slap 4" on your chest, 3" on each arm, muscularize your waist, build speedy legs—using the exact same secrets I gave to the champs! I don't care if today, you own the scraggiest, flabbiest, funniest body—whether you're short or tall, young or not-so-young. I guarantee you that virtually overnight with my championship-proven methods you'll experience a muscle-building miracle! And for the first time in your life men will envy you, women admire you because at last, your body will bring you fame instead of shame!

Remember, your body is too precious to trust into the hands of amateurs, phonies and profiteers — follow me and you follow the champs I've trained in the safest, most scientific, time-tested, result-producing course of all time! Let me prove it to you— send for your 2 FREE GIFTS which reveal the greatest muscle-building secrets ever put into print! Don't let this once-in-a-life-time limited opportunity slip by. MAIL COUPON BELOW TO ME TODAY. You have nothing to lose but your weakness!

JOE WEIDER — Personal Trainer of "Mr. America," "Mr. Universe" and other perfect men title winners since 1936. Over 2,000,000 successful students!

"I CHALLENGE ANY TEN PHYSICAL INSTRUCTORS COMBINED TO PROVE THAT I DO NOT TURN OUT MORE "PERFECT MEN" TITLE WINNERS IN ONE YEAR THAN THEY HAVE DONE IN THEIR ENTIRE CAREERS!"

MAIL COUPON FOR 2 FREE GIFTS

JOE WEIDER, Dept. 64-90B1
Trainer of the Champions since 1936
531-32nd Street, Union City, N. J. 07087

Dear Joe: Shoot the works! Thanks for making available to me FREE your Exclusive and Patented Secret Gifts—that I can use instantly at home to build myself a handsome, rugged body! I'm enclosing only 25c to cover handling and mailing charges! I'm under no further obligation in any way.

Name..Age.......

Address...

City................State.........Zip.......
(Please Print Clearly)

THIS IS AN OUTRIGHT GIFT . . . YOU'RE UNDER NO OBLIGATION . . . NOTHING TO BUY!

△ source **Man's Action**

That's Sexy! ————— 79

everyone should experience
something new...

THE WETTER THE BETTER

Jennifer Jon
Andrea True
Angel Barret

Produced by Eri
Edw

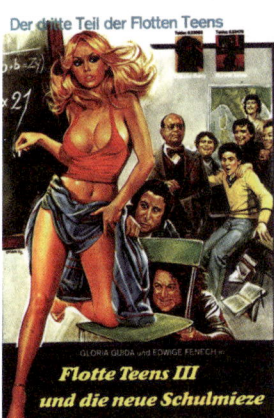

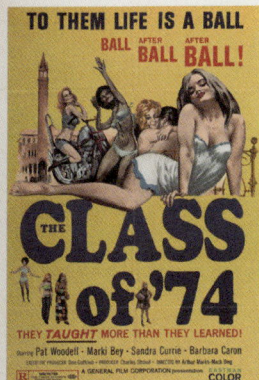

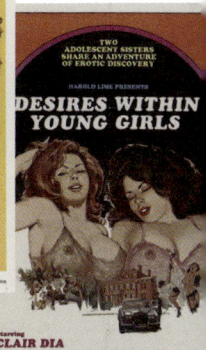

ELTUNTERGA
EN AM RANDE DES NERVENZUSAMM

© Germany picture by Adam Tappman

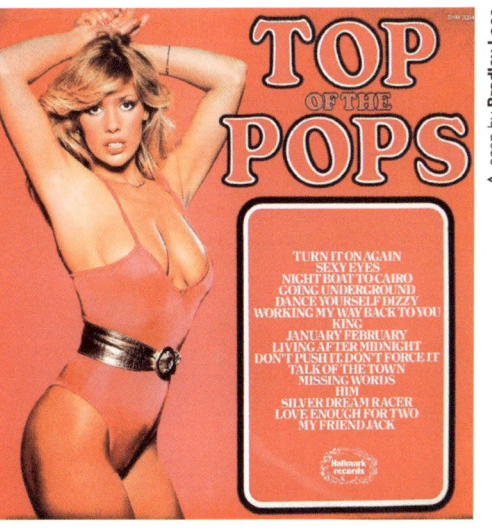

TOP OF THE POPS

TURN IT ON AGAIN
SEXY EYES
NIGHT BOAT TO CAIRO
GOING UNDERGROUND
DANCE YOURSELF DIZZY
WORKING MY WAY BACK TO YOU
KING
JANUARY FEBRUARY
LIVING AFTER MIDNIGHT
DON'T PUSH IT, DON'T FORCE IT
TALK OF THE TOWN
MISSING WORDS
HIM
SILVER DREAM RACER
LOVE ENOUGH FOR TWO
MY FRIEND JACK

full bodied

orchy

lets the taste come through

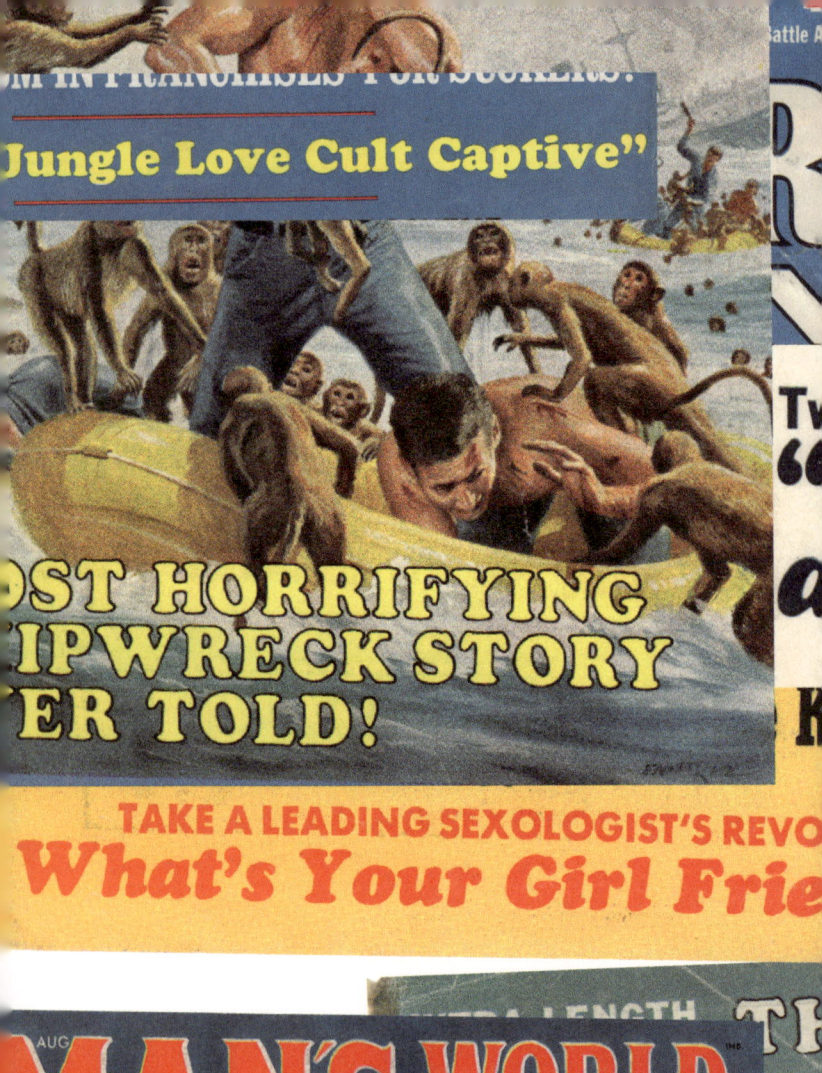

"Jungle Love Cult Captive"

OST HORRIFYING IPWRECK STORY ER TOLD!

TAKE A LEADING SEXOLOGIST'S REVO

What's Your Girl Frie

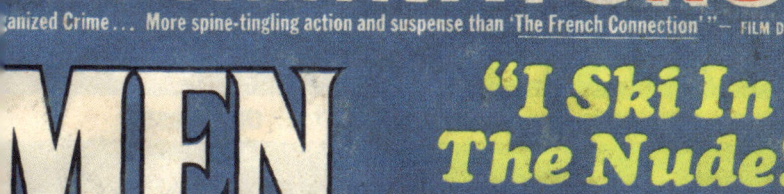

MEN
LY

60¢

"I Ski In The Nude!"

...A "Snow Job" Girl Reveals Her Sex Life

● ● ●

esbians Talk About Their Life

Ve Make Love We Please"

T
D

FOREIGN "MINICARS" - OUR HIGHWAYS' #1 MENAC

● ● ●

ONARY NEW "INSTANT SEX QUIZ"!

's "Bedroom Profile"?

TREASURE RAPER

(Hitler's gold was guarded by sharks for 25 years, waiting for R
the man with the guts and the blonde to rip it out and fight fo

FOR

JERRY DALY

CHOPPER HAW

"MY MOTHER LIVES IN CINCINNATI"

No. D-1 .... "THE WRESTLERS" .... A modern version of the renowned classic statue of Hercules & Gladiate. The original is in the Vecchia Palace in Florence, Italy. 10" tall in antique travertine finish duratone. A must for collectors of erotic exotica and vice versa! And a conversation piece to say the leat! **Each $11.95**

No. 7220 A Reproduction of an antique locket and chain. Holds two pictures. Gold plated. Chain is approx. 22" long. Locket measures 1" x ¾". **Each $6.50**

D-2 CLASSIC TORSO ... An exciting original, provocative sculpture created exclusively for Mother by David Damon. Hand cast in duractone, antique ivory or jade finish. Approx. 9" tall. A must for the collector of the beautiful and unusual. **Each ... $14.95**

No. 7238 .... PAISLEY FLARES for men & women ... comfortable & colorful lounging pants ... new & neat. Drawstring waist, predshrunk cotton. Men's sizes S,M,L,XL. Women's sizes Petite, S,M,L. **Each $12.95**

No. 7220-M ... 22" chain with reproduction of an antique Frozen Hunting Horn. Aponte already 1" x 1", gold plated antique finish. **Each $6.50**

No. 7252 ... MUSLIN FLARES for men & women. Drawstring waist, unbleached, preshrunk. Men's sizes S,M,L,XL. Women's sizes Petite, S,M,L. **Each $8.95**

No. 7204 ... CAVALIER SHIRT for men or women. Preshrunk muslin. Sizes S,M,L. **Each $13.95**

No.7248 SENSUOUS SLIP-ON WIDEPANTS for men & women. Soft, unlined cotton pants in colorful tapestry print with elastic waist band. Men's sizes S,M,L,XL. Women's sizes Petite, S,M,L. **Each $12.95**

*All pants unhemmed (alter them as you wish).

No. 7253 ... MUSLIN WIDEPANTS for men & women. Elastic waistband, pre shrunk. * Men's sizes S,M,L,XL. Women's sizes Petite, S,M,L. **Each $8.95**

No. 7265 ... MOTHER'S LOGO BAG. 21" long x 24" wide heavy canvas. **Each $6.00**

Add $1 shipping charge per order. Calif. residents add sales tax. Send check or money order. No C.O.D.'s please. BankAmericard, Master Charge welcome. Include Account No. Fascinating catalog ... 50¢ — FREE with your order.

MOTHER, INC. P.O. BOX 707, DEPT. AD-9 SOUTH LAGUNA, CA 92677

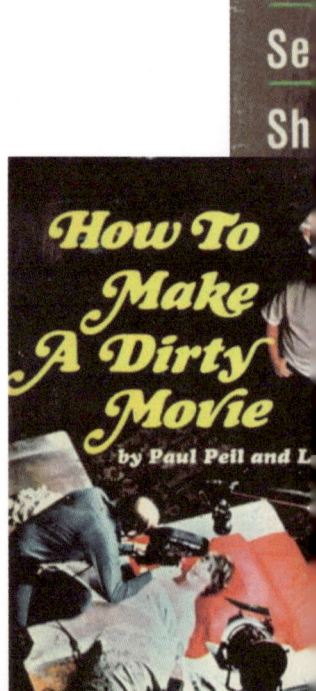

R 12

PK107
$1.00

Adam

Vashington
een
Blues

Schedule

lack

sochist

g
nical

A si
that
Sex

"A sign that says 'Sex' has to stand out, but not too prominently. People's eyes get attracted by the word, but their minds make them look away at the same time."

C. Jansen
Sex Shop Owner

Wha
Che

t's so

ap?

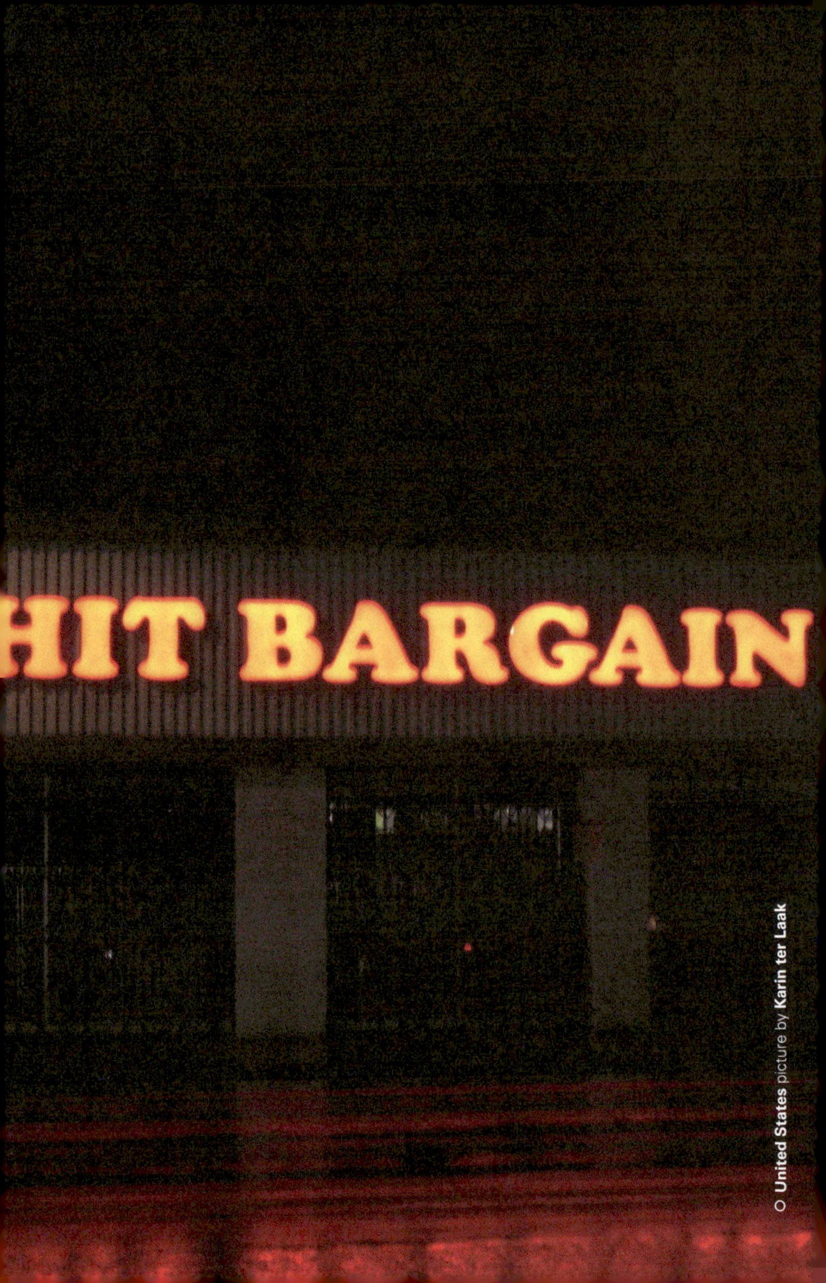

○ **United States** picture by **Karin ter Laak**

It's Common

It's Friendly

It's Popular

It's Everywhere

It's Simple

It Sells

**All Bargains,
nothing more**

MINI
OUTIQUE

△ **Germany** picture by **Adam Tappman**

ARUNEE HOUSE

THAI FOOD

THAI–CHINESE
FOOD TO GO

© France picture by Ward Nicolaas

▽ **United States** picture by **Adam Tappman**

we sell

Ame

App

Venice
Beach

VENI
BEA

© United States picture by Karin ter Laak

Serious Injury • Auto • Wrongful Death • Traffic Tickets

ACCIDENTS

SE HABLA ESPAÑOL   NO RECOVERY - NO FEE

Dover Danialpour - Attorney At Law
Joseph Pourshalimy - Attorney At Law

(310) 444-0055

* **United States** picture by **Karin ter Laak**

The big cha

"The big characters are clear and attract attention. That's why I chose this font. Besides that, it doesn't make it too classy, like a restaurant in which you can eat a three-course meal. This is a diner, you know."

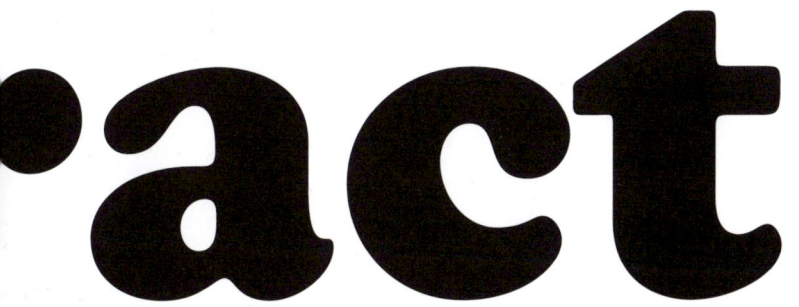

I. Gunaydin
Owner of Masada döner shop

Wh
so A

at's
rty?

y Other Typeface

Comic Sans

It's Imaginative

It's Original

It's Immortal

It's Reproducible

It's Camp

It's Groovy

All Font,
no Fuss

△ **United States** by **Michael Babcock**

Cooper
Black

1924 O B Cooper

★ **Japan** concept & design **Masashi Kawamura** production & design **Itaru Yonenaga / No Control Air** picture by **Munetaka Tokuyama**

○ The Netherlands by Reimar Kuies

▽ shirt by **Unknown**

△ **United Kingdom** by **Edward Quarmby**

FROM THE SUN COME THE FIRE-PEOPLE
TO INCINERATE ALL MANKIND!

The CREMATORS

GREAT BALLS OF FIRE:
SCORCHING!
RAVAGING!
ENGULFING!

aaaaaaa **edding** transfer
ref. 3223
aaaaaa 5mm
18pt.   COOPER BLACK
aabbbbbbbcccccccc
ccdddddddddddee
eeeeeeeeeeeeeeee
eeeeeeeeeeffff:
gggggghhhhhhh!
iiiiiiiiiiiiiiiijjjj
jkkkkkkkkkllll
llllllllllmmmm?
mmmm nnnnnn
nnnnnnnnoooo:
ooooooooooppp!
ppppppqqqqqrrrr
rrrrrrrrrrsssss!
ssssssttttttt;
uuuuuuuuuu
wx
zzzz
ßßß
,,,,,,
«»
;;;::1111
33333444
66666777

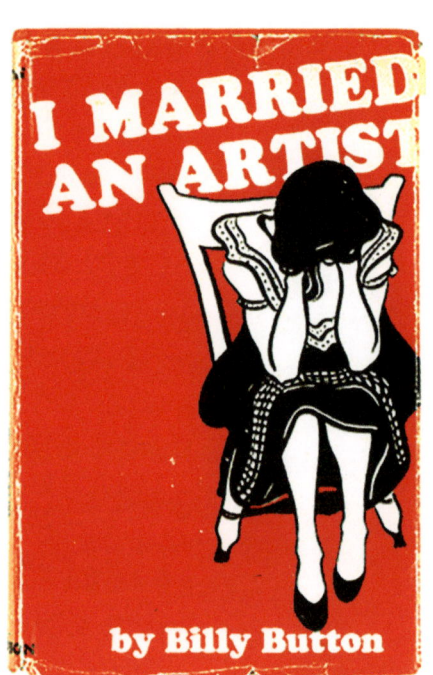

▽ United States publisher **Open City, Inc.**

shirt by **Urban Outfitters**

© United States by Jeremy Backo

cooper black
70's icon

▽ **United States** picture by **Christy Medellin**

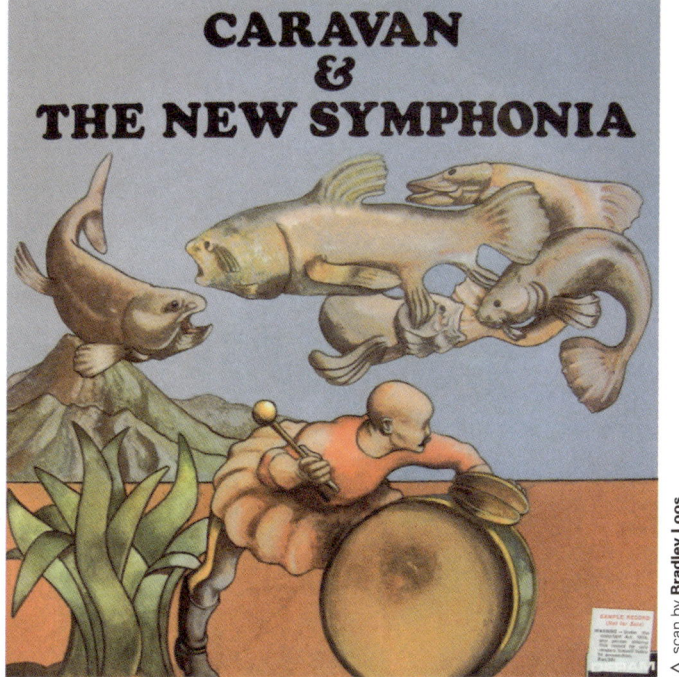

CARAVAN
&
THE NEW SYMPHONIA

t's
easy

"Cooper Black's bold, confident and distinct appearance has made the brand recognisable and associated with 'easy'. Its soft friendly curves have given a warm personality to the 'easy' businesses.

Cooper Black sells not only things we now consider to be retro and classic, such as Kickers or Spacehoppers, but also anything intended to be warm, fuzzy, homely, reliable and reassuring, like easyJet. The lettering on the sides of planes had rarely implied fun before easyJet tried it, and so strong is this typographic branding that no one has successfully imitated it."

The easyGroup
Brand Manual
www.easy.com

Wha
Las

t's so
ting?

Chiliburger

Bacon Burger

Hot Dog

Chili Dog

Cheese Dog

Chili Cheese Dog

Grilled Cheese

Grilled Ham

Grilled Ham & Ch

Pastrami

BBQ Beef

Steak

Bacon Let. & Tom.

Pattie Melt

Tuna Melt

French Fries

Tuna Salad

Egg Salad

It's Suitable

It's Readable

It's Characteristic

It's Everlasting

It's Great

It's the Type
of all Times

The Beach Boys Pet Sounds

Wouldn't It Be Nice/You Still Bel[...]
That's Not Me/Dont Talk (Put Yo[...]
I'm Waiting For The Day/Let's Go[...]
God Only Knows/I Know There's[...]
I Just Wasn't Made For These Ti[...]

No. 178 June 19th, 1971   EVERY THURSDAY   Price **3p**

Twinkle

The picture paper specially for little girls

TWINKLE often feeds the goats
On her Uncle David's farm.
But this kid likes to help himself
From the basket on her arm.

ERS, OPPRESSED NATIONS AND PEOPLE OF THE WORLD, UNITE!

ED PATRIOT
AN TÍRGHRÁTHÓIR DEARG

...ly of the
Party of Ireland
...inist)

Vol. 5 No. 42-43
Dec. 1st & 14th 1976
price 30p

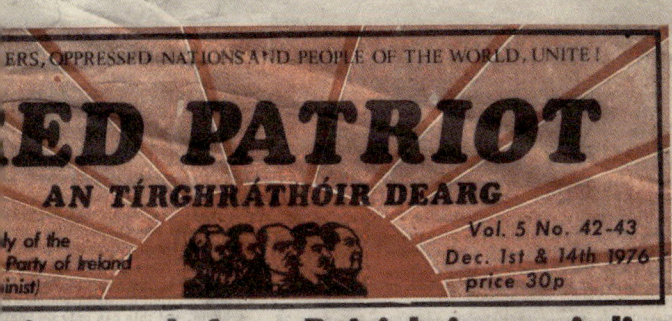

...nise to defeat British imperialist aggression and plunder
...nise to defeat the Irish monopoly ...apitalists north and south

...ears now the British imperialist
...been spreading rumours about
...thdrawal from northern Ireland.
...propaganda - they first of all
...nd then reply to themselves,
...a 'debate' on the issue. We are
...g told that the British imper-
...dering withdrawing, and fuel
...this by the British spokesmen
...tinuously denying such a poss-

...ssue of withdrawal, which is
...some left wing and patriotic

...aspects to this issue. First,
...rialists are raising it straight-
...se they have no intention what-
...ng their imperialist aggression
...reland, north and south, and are
...the people by making it appear

jurisdiction over the north at all, its "Govern-
ment of Ireland Act" which legalises the annex-
ation of northern Ireland to Britain, total defeat
of the British imperialist armed forces, cess-
ation of all British imperialist financial and
industrial activities in Ireland north and south
and complete halt to all their political interference
and back-door dealing. In short British imper-
ialism has to GET OUT OF IRELAND ! Nothing
short of this will answer the just demands of
the people. Nothing short of this will stop ex-
ploitation of the Irish people and allow them to
establish a workers and small farmers independ-
ent state, a People's Republic. All this talk
about withdrawal that the British imperialists are
carrying on has nothing to do with such a demand.
What the demand for withdrawal at best means
is either the removal of most of the troops and
the reduction of the imperialist forces in the
north to a small garrison, the way they were

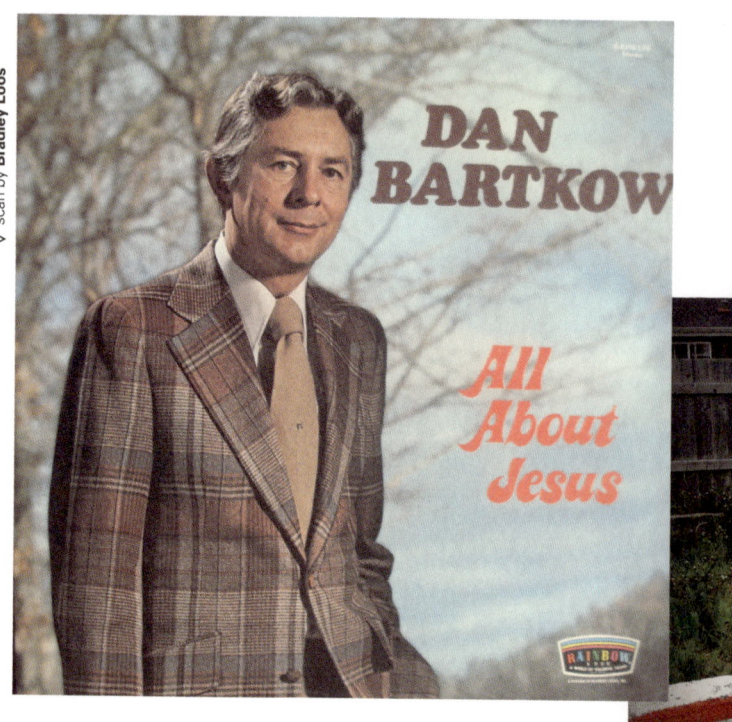

△ **United States** picture by **Susanna Tron**

How High Am I?

▶ A JOURNAL ◀

GENIUS IDEAS · DRAWINGS
STUFF YOU DON'T WANT TO FORGET

△ publisher **Chronicle Books**

▽ **United States** advertisement for **Burger King**

▽ scan by **Bradley Loos**

Dancing Machine

JACKSON 5IVE

▽ **United States** picture by **Scott Schiller**

▽ **United States** picture by **Karin ter Laak**

▽ **Sweden** picture by James Anderson

○ **United States** picture by Scott Schiller

▽ **United Kingdom** picture by Rob Waller

Welcome to
830
AMSTERDAM AVE.
HOUSES

MANAGED BY FREDERICK DOUGLAS

PREZZO!D

Dürüm

DÖNER

© Germany picture by Elisa Daugello

△ **Germany** by **Modern Fashion Apparel Supply**

You CAN earn far more money – accept one of these FREE Books
and in simple language find out HOW!

IF you want quicker promotion or a new job, you *must* read one of these remarkable books. Simply choose YOUR pet subject and we will send you a valuable free Guide, giving full details of our Appointments and Advisory Depts., and the widest range of modern, pay - winning Postal Courses.

NO OBLIGATION

If you earn less than £25 a week, you owe it to yourself to find out how we can help you. Fill in the Coupon and post it today. We will then send you an absorbingly interesting career book — FREE and without obligation.

Accountancy
Advertising
Aero Eng.
Agriculture
Architecture
Article Writing
Auto. Eng.
Banking
Book-keeping
Building
  (all branches)
Business
  Management
Carpentry &
  Joinery
Cartooning
Chemical Eng.
Civil Eng.
Civil Service
Clerk of Works
Commercial Art
Cost Account'cy
Customs Officer
Decorating
Die & Press Tools
Diesel Eng.
Draughtsman'ship
Electrical Eng.
Electronics
Fashion Drawing
Fiction Writing
Foundry Work
A.M.I.Mech.E.
A.M.I.C.E.
A.M.I.Chem.E.

Garage M'ment
General
Heating and
  Ventilat
Illumin'g Eng.
Instrument
  Te
Jig & Tool De
Journalism
Local Govt.
Maint'ance En
Marine Eng.
Mathematics
Mechanical En
Mechanics
Metallurgy
Mining
Motor Repair
Municipal Eng
Office M'men
Pattern
  Making (En
Personnel
  Manageme
Plumbing
Police Career
Practical Radi
Press Tool W
Petroleum Te
Prison Service
Production En
B.Sc. (Eng.)
B.Sc. (Econ.)
A.M.B.I.M.

Psychology
Education

CITY & GUILDS, GEN. CERT

Free!

FREE HANDBOOKS
FOR AMBITIOUS PEOPLE

POST COUPON

The School of Careers,
House, 29-31, Wright's Lan
Please send me a FREE Car

NAME ....

ADDRESS ....
....
....

SUBJECT OF
INTEREST ....

The School of Careers
In Association with British Institute of Engineering Technolog

ookfest
urning,
-busting
t of fun.

**Oxfam
Bookfest**
4 - 18 July '09
www.oxfam.org.uk/schools

Oxfam

△ **United Kingdom** advertisement for **Oxfam Novib**

Every book we sell can help provide much needed shelter

Bookshop volunteers

Spend some time volunteering with us and you'll soon find out just how rewarding a book can be. That's because the money we make selling donated books helps to fund our fight against poverty and suffering. So as well as growing your skills and retail experience, you'll have a positive impact on millions of lives around the world.

For more information and to pick up an application form, pop inside for a chat.

www.oxfam.org.uk/jobs

Oxfam works with others to overcome poverty and suffering.

Oxfam

Be Humankind

△ **United Kingdom** advertisement for **Oxfam Novib**

SECURITY

GOLD IN YOUR PURSE
When there's
SILVER IN YOUR HAIR

A comparatively small sum set aside each year for an
Equitable Retirement Annuity will guarantee you a fixed
monthly income of $100, $200, $300 or $500 *for life*,
beginning at any age after 50. Suitable for the individual,
or for the joint support of a man and wife. If preferred,
the annuity may be purchased by a lump-sum payment.

THE EQUITABLE
LIFE ASSURANCE SOCIETY OF THE UNITED STATES

THOMAS I. PARKINSON, *President*
393 SEVENTH AVENUE, NEW YORK, N. Y.

*The Retirement Annuity is but one of the
many forms of Self-Income and Life Insur-
ance service available through The Equitable.*

TO THE EQUITABLE, 393 7th Ave., New York, N. Y.

Please send me booklet explaining your Retirement Income
plans. My age is_____   14-G

Name_____

Address_____

LIFE

'68

The Incredible Year

SPECIAL ISSUE

T... ...een
f... ...in space,
a... ...utlines of
N... ...th America

JANUARY 10 · 1969 · 40¢

△ **United States** publisher **LIFE**

Stevie Wonder
down
to earth

A PLACE IN THE SUN
BANG BANG * THANK YOU LOVE
MR. TAMBOURINE MAN
HEY LOVE * SIXTEEN TONS
DOWN TO EARTH
SYLVIA * THE LONESOME ROAD
MY WORLD IS EMPTY WITHOUT YOU
ANGEL BABY (Don't You Ever Leave Me)
BE COOL, BE CALM (And Keep Yourself Together)

TAMLA

△ scan by **Bradley Loos**

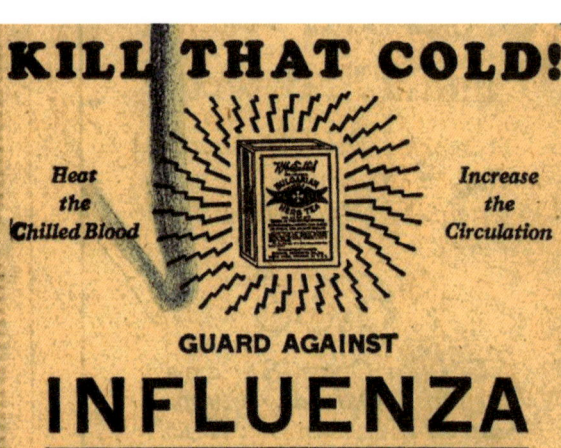

KILL THAT COLD!

Heat
the
Chilled Blood

Increase
the
Circulation

GUARD AGAINST

INFLUENZA

DON'T FIND YOURSELF SICK-A-BED DURING THE HOLIDAY SEASON!
Get yourself and family in physical shape to fight off Winter Ills.
Do the Right Thing Now...Take a Cupful of

Steaming Hot

BULGARIAN HERB TEA

The rich juices brewed from the herbs, roots, barks, leaves, plants and flowers, taken steaming hot at bedtime, assist nature to quickly break up a cold and guard against Grippe, Influenza or Pneumonia. Take a cupful twice a week during these danger months...it will cleanse your system and put you in shape to fight attacks of flu and cold germs. See your druggist. He can honestly recommend Bulgarian Herb Tea. Do not fool with a cold.

Trial size, 25c—Medium Family Size, 75c—Large Family Size, $1.25

▷ United States advertisement for Bulgarian Herb Tea

Coo
Blac

"Cooper Black was always meant to be a novelty typeface, but unlike other pre-war novelty faces, it continues to be used in the same way it was intended: as a friendly advertising headliner. The connotations may be a bit different now, but Oswald Cooper created something that serves its purpose well after it was created. The same thing that can be claimed by Garamond, Bodoni, and Jenson."

Stephen Coles
FontShop International
www.fontshop.com

COOPER BLACK

COOPE

COOPER

Black 36 Point

Black 48 Poin

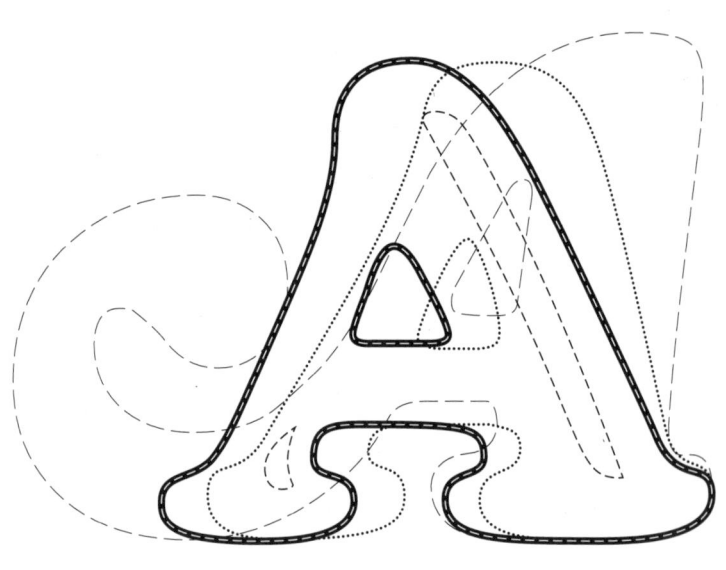

Meant to be seen rather than rea

Cooper Black is a heavy thick-stroked typeface with rounded serifs that initially enjoyed about 20 years of popularity in both metal and wood applications. The typeface is drawn as an extra-bold weight of Oswald Cooper's earlier typeface Cooper Old Style (1919), the result of Barnhart Brothers & Spindler type foundry representatives Richard N. McArthur and Charles R. Murray. They saw the biggest potential in the super-bold advertising lettering that would become Cooper Black, but agreed that a roman weight old style should be executed first, the logical progenitor to a family of related types.

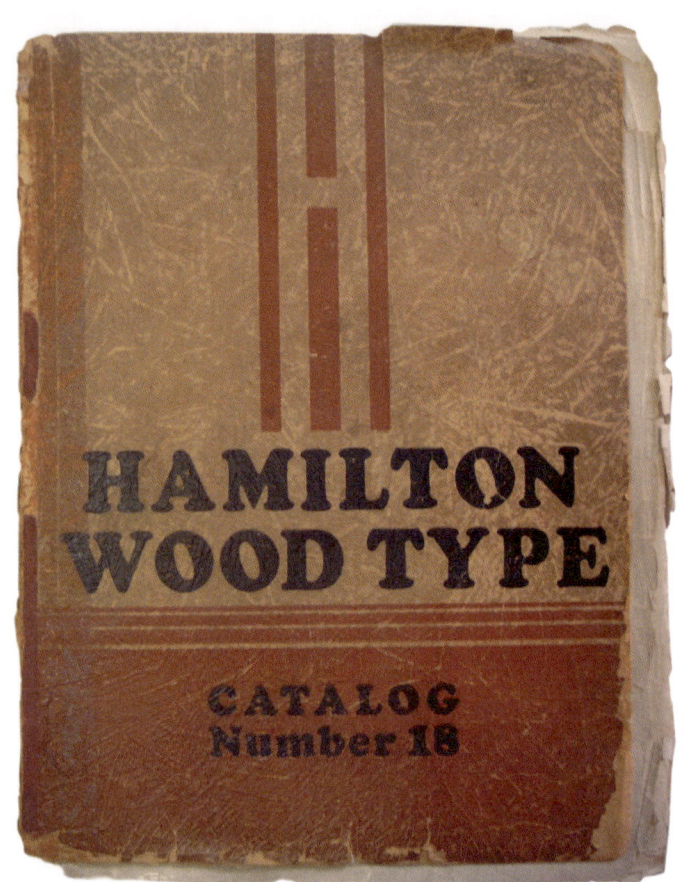

Cooper Old Style was originally released as a non-kerning typeface, which offered limited use for type-setting. Oz Cooper was never quite happy with the copious amount of 'air' around the typeface's characters. Cooper redrew the lowercase characters multiple times, toying with the rounded forms of the **m** and **n**, and engaged in a lively debate with Barnhart Bros. & Spindler's general manager Richard N. McArthur over the final form as McArthur requested that the typeface be drawn bolder and bolder. Cooper originally drew the figures the same width as the **M** of the font, but revised them to the width of the **N** at the request of McArthur.

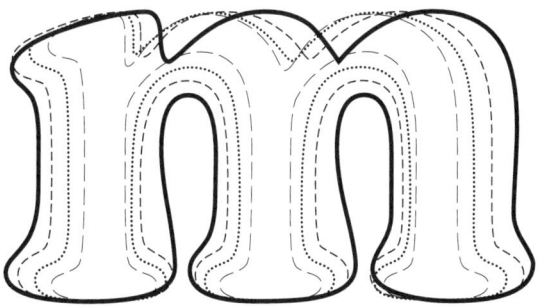

Though not based on a single historic model, Cooper Black exhibits influences of Art Nouveau, Art Deco, and the Machine Age. The flowing outer contours create forms that are both strong and soft, making Cooper Black an extremely flexible font. The absence of sharp corners made it very well suited to wood-type. It was quickly adopted by the Hamilton Company and used for the cover of their **Wood-Type Catalog No.18**.

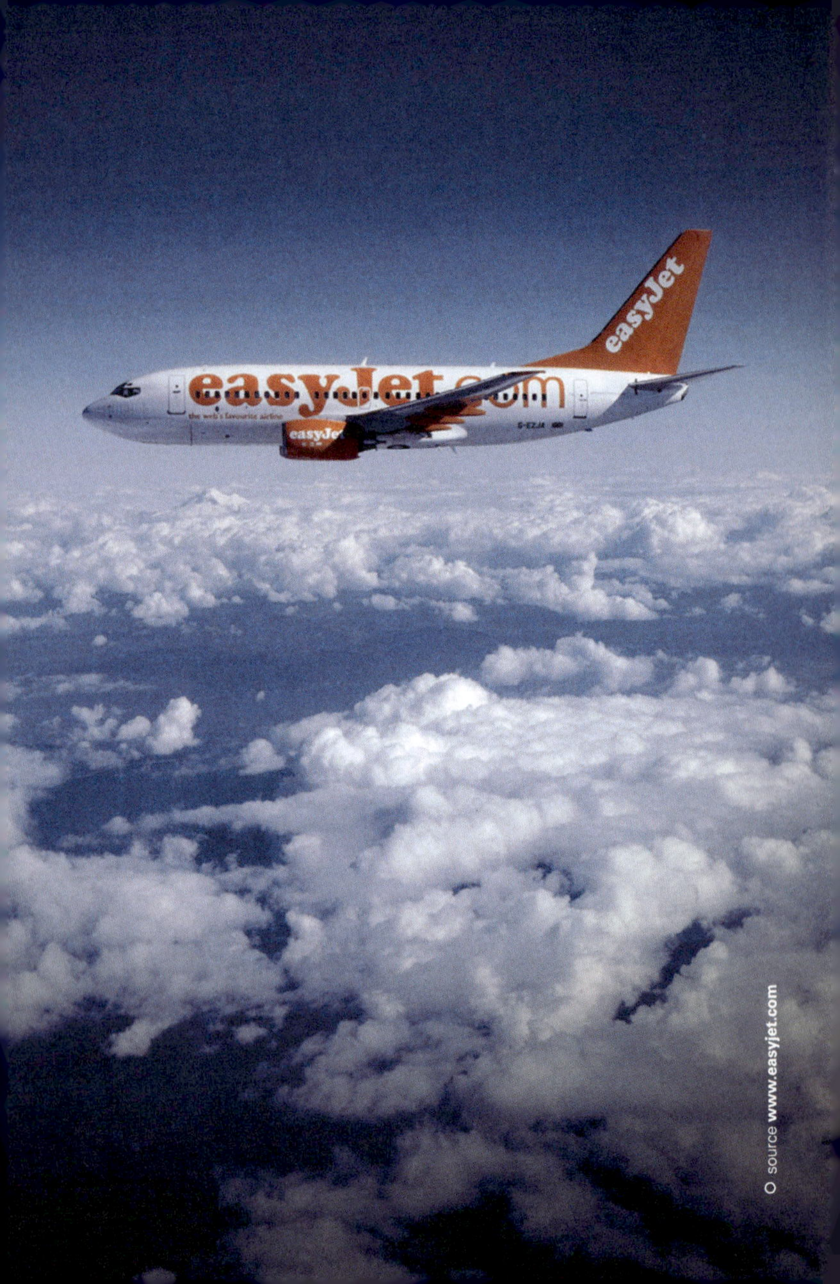

© source www.easyjet.com

The lack of contrast in the design calls for using this font on a clearly divergent background. The little nicks at the tops and bases of letters give the font a solid flat weight on a page; without them, the type would always have appeared to roll away. For a font with such a thickset look, it retains a remarkably unthreatening demeanour. This is due in part to its stout and pudgy descenders, its large lower-case letters in relation to its capitals, and the limited white peering through the counters of the **a**, **b**, **d**, **e** and **g**. It is usually employed quite bunched up, since excessive spacing between letters would make it break up very fast, confusing the eye.

Cooper Black looks best from afar, as **easyJe**t recognised. Its weakness as a text font is immediately clear, however. At small sizes, Cooper Black is legible but not very readable. Then again, some type is meant to be seen rather than read. Cooper Black is one of those typefaces.

sources

www.ianlynam.com/type-design/cooper-text/

typophile.com/node/15256

wikipedia.org/wiki/Oswald_Bruce_Cooper

Cooper Black **Regular**

abcdefghijklm
nopqrstuvxyz

Cooper Black **Regular Capitals**

ABCDEFGHIJ
KLMNOPQRS
TUVXYZ

Cooper Black **Hightlight**

ABCDEFGHIJ
KLMNOPQRS
TUVXYZ

Cooper Black **Italic**

abcdefghijklm
nopqrstuvxyz

Cooper Black **Italic Capitals**

ABCDEFGHIJ
KLMNOPQRS
TUVXYZ

Cooper Black **Italic Swash**

ABCDEFGHIJ
KLMNOPQRS
TUVXYZ

Relu
ode

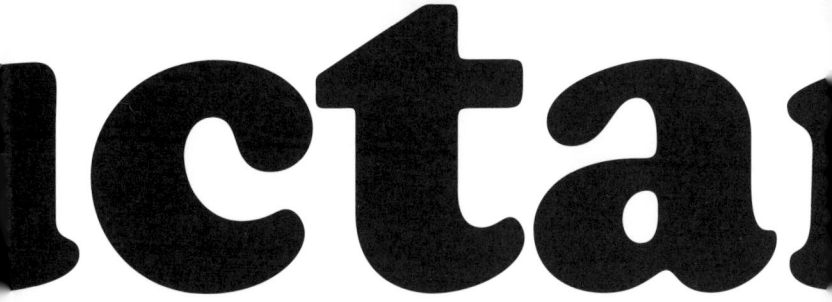

"Reluctant ode to Cooper Black. What do Tootsie Rolls, *M*A*S*H*, *The Odd Couple*, *Garfield*, Frank Zappa's 1966 debut album *Freak Out!* and David Bowie's *The Rise and Fall of Ziggy Stardust and the Spiders from Mars* all have in common? They all use Cooper Black, the font we all know but never use. At least I don't.

Developed in the 1920s by Oswald Cooper, Cooper Black is a like a stout, pudgy friend: thick, dark, and friendly. I can't say I really *like* Cooper Black. The fact is, I've never, ever *used* Cooper Black. But who can deny its like-ability? Who doesn't want to be friends with Cooper Black? Have a damn beer with Cooper Black? I know I do."

by Scott Citron
Director at Large, Type Directors Club
www.tdc.org

Knock knock
Who's there?

Cooper Black!
Cooper who?

Cooper Black is black,
I want my
babyface back